AF225147

Previous publications from Mica Press:

Amores by Clive Wilmer

Orengo by Nicholas Orengo

Leslie Bell

Archipelagos

First published in Great Britain in 2012 by
Mica Press
2 Paget Road, Wivenhoe
Colchester, Essex CO7 9DT
Later (2013 -)
47 Belle Vue Road, Wivenhoe
Colchester, Essex CO7 9LD.

Leslie Bell asserts his moral right to be identified
as the author of this book.

ISBN 978-1-869848-01-9

2nd impression

Some poems in this book have previously appeared in *The Rialto*, and on the web sites privatewww.essex.ac.uk/~lbell and www.lezbell.com (also known as www.versicules.com). Many have been heard at poetry readings in Wivenhoe, Colchester and Prague.

Thanks are due to John Wakeman, Michael Mackmin, Clive Wilmer, John Muckle, L.J.T Barnard, Chris and Sara Lord, Mandy Llewellyn, and David Charleston. Special thanks to my partner Kate Nevard and her children Gus and Anna.

Table of Contents

Might, Right: the Desert

The 4th Arab-Israeli War, 1973

On sudden tracks lead horsemen ride
In a parallel wilderness
Their fellows to each one just
Thundershadows flying scarves of dust
Shaken from heavy hooves
To the waterbright, spectral walls.
What they fled in a world of skies,
Whose axes cross where visor joins with helm,
Their narrowing glance advanced into the waste
Annihilation: scattering before them
All angles there that threatened or might brim
Over their horses' necks.

    The horsemen's shadows blackened and grew small
    Like images of silence in the din
    Of heavy onwardness.

    The riders urge their steeds together, then apart,
    Desolation, a red-rimmed banner, formed
    From the dust shook out behind their harness.

Till the horizons analyzed by force
And barbed with vanishing points become a brim,
Mercy and Grief
Ride with the warriors, nowhere to be found.

(Heroically)

These were his designs in life
To paint a picture, find a wife
To write a book of poetry
About the mystery
That never cloyed.
He'd written just enough to tease
His wife and he near enemies
The pictures
Were brief departures
For the void
Until a lump of shapeless clay
Produced by ages of decay
Was all he had
Among the mad
And so employed
Upon the grave's own synonym
He made a Janus out of him
Both ways facing,
Not embracing
But not annoyed.
And on the potter's wheel he raised
Humble hollows fired and glazed
Voids attained
And lightly stained
He had enjoyed
The last ambition of his thirtieth year
A year that closes on his lust and fear
And tentative
Now, could live
(A humanoid).

The Jeweller's Mistress

Pondering her integrity at a feast,
he on a sudden knew how to unsay
the sour chills and acrimonial heats
that made equivalent
                            inclines of her days.
He took the cruet; there his mind digressed
on formal amethyst and orthoclaze.

Ziggurat

Standing on the ridge of dawn, how the day seems
the sun in your heads hotter than powerful chilli
the lady in red sprawling the gate- legged table
of your untold dream, /and afternoon went
endlessly /scribbling Spain Caribbean Spain /
till the ludicrous query when? when? strikes
and goes on striking as the pipes knock -
and you quench the hot irons / of your blood in
laughter / cooler than jasmine, quivering ripples
hiss /outer than Curaçao, Cuba, Calibania,
shunting you rockingly free of the driftstuff /tide-edge
past pure cares of continents, /crystal-dreary islands
over magnetic fallen empire beds where Geminid showers
/
streamed astral messages kinder than comet-tails
whipping laconic limb-laden dust-clouds aglow
until delicately ionized
in the pauseless passage of parsecs
you rub noses in the minutely swaying colossal
ANTI-UNIVERSE, where anti-buds and tendrils
(globed in an anti-glass blown anti-by glaziers)
respire droplets anti-ly green as puke
and you notice the travelling strangeness vitally lacks
one component essentially: the print-out sprouts your
names.
You're home! By all that's wonderful, at home, out here!
But how on earth - on anti-earth, that is -
are you at home, and how to get back here?
But it's far too late to think of that, and see,
the anti-creature up there on a stalk
is a sore throat, right outside its neck
and - oh my fathers, how did it get out -
a street lamp, minus electricity.

No Inventory Can Do Her Justice

The salt in an egg-cup
screwy lid under a flowerpot
the banknotes in a clothespeg
cupful of pipe and pens
the fankled hank of wool
yeast in tablet form
the words in a book

In one week I bought a painting, read 4 plays,talked about   holidays,
exams, the weather, Poland. I have seen herons
and other dawn raiders, made concrete, made a garden,
been painted by two women, painted a windowsill and a
doorframe, had a haircut, spoken to an old friend for the first time in
ten years, been to the seaside, planted irises,
found a lost hammer, received and read a letter and a book, stayed
awake all one night, seen some paintings of cows, wielded a hosepipe,
drenching your son in my anger.

Can answer some
                    like why spiders
do not catch in their webs
with a higher tensile strength than steel

but why do days
open inward on epitaphs,
nights open like fans onto patterns
and only the dream you wake from is recalled?
The real language was a dialectal burr
Or forgotten, like a Justice on a plinth.

Demolition lunch hour

Raylow was at work inside. Seven light bulbs hung on one stalk for the hurt brain he had. It was anyway not needed. Squawks and shins barked in a draconian drought of release. Raylow's stultified breathing was a light dusting of sound like wind in a hedge but close up you could see the reiterated shocks of words had parted from their meanings like warts from a skin drilled with silver nitrate pencil. The broken dance of insteps outwith the walls enclosing rubble was co-ordinated and contained. Segments of light-ale drinkers' heads carried down the step, slogged in a zig-zag of peer effrontery, and got lifted with the man under them by will and muscle in a roar no seg of thought could recognizably emit.

Rime

The bedroom window-pane was frosted white
When I and my good lover said good-night:
Intense our heat was, but in morning's flame,
The ice was on the window still. I came
To think human fire, love and fury
Are but sparks a winter's snow will bury.

The Non-Affair

Throckmorton, in your clean retreat I see
my shabby loudness turned to policy.
A grass stalk parted with its stem
and at the joint unsheathed a white
end of fresh cellulose to chew on, sweet,
nutritionless and spatulate.

Nature red in poem after poem

awaits man, this morning.
"A serviceable villain -" grin, slash
"What di yi doew wi them," stab,
grab, twist. In a dark cranny
anyone will take moonshine
for a piece of Christmas cake
and peek at the bright human forest -
"Come and see, they're different!"

That's putting it mildly. Sometimes I put my work
down on a light-veined marble top. Slabs of people
come past with a clatter. United, isn't it?

Di-doom, di-doom, a merry boat,
While greasy God don't hear a lot.

Annual Incident

Woken by flashing light at 8 a.m.
drank some water. To depart from fact,
he breakfasted on the tip of rubbish,
cigarette ends, gaudy present husks
stuck up the cards and hoovered. The signs
with which he blocked the broken window said
"Job Black Spot", "Sea Scouts", till replaced
with lucent polythene, cleanly and discreet.
With nothing more than usual now on the floor
the bloody fool felt like a guest himself,
entered the street: birds hopped, and others walked
rapt in a new year solitude that mild weather
like lost bugs shaken out of a mat of car hugs
out of the tartan of kissing spread criss-cross the year.
Cloud, and the lifting birds' heads capped with blue
seemed standardized as a steady job inside
the telecommunications citadel red box,
and local by comparison with speech.
Poor speech, too instantaneous to be real,
too comfortable to comfort, quickly sieved
for un-adaptable crumbs of greater urgency,
loss between past and present like the night
still to live and speed along and look
past Britain like a fallen Christmas tree
presence gone from the root of the star of the sea.

Signor Sourpuss

He saw, to her he'd never been defenceless
The storms of tears that marrow-shook him slack
Seemed to her witness known from raising children
Something as oedipal as stark attack.

She could see only in the print he'd 'prenticed
She'd not be bested by his luckless lack,
And, more than her bon ton of tart rejoinder,
Beauty enjoining reason answered back

It was fair slaughter, it was better reason
That never hinted beauty, being it.
It was not reason that gave beauty answer
By the gob churl that gallant lady fit.

When I Had Lust and She Did it Requite

In you secure, my freedom without fear
Grew senselessly outward from you my dear,
Till it, a world too large, collapsed within,
Freedom grew dark and honesty a sin.

You insecure, kissing became a stone
By which two weary heads lay close alone.
Worn down by tears it gave way with a groan
And our two heads other than speech had none.

Freedom to be not free cannot exist.
Freedom to love with lies cannot subsist.
Love must precede, or freedom to love is
Hollow and roaring, though still the thing it is.

Love is to freedom as water is to stone,
The world is water over bedrock bone.
Freedom with freedom builds, stone joined to stone
And to love is to love, a single crystal grown.

Tryst

A black sound reached
my arms and tongue
today, then sank
into my breast, with the fallen
sound of
        old, unlike, metals.
In your garden is
the green leaves' bride and bridegroom
as here the lilac throws down rot.
I do the alphabet to
my skull-white card.

The Talisman and Psalms 22, 44, 88

Heartbreak and moonshine
flood the impalpable sands of human
hearts deserted made for
work and happiness. Lord
God of Hosts, give over your
implacable demand for
psalms: your wolfish hungered
teeth crunching the grain of tears,
clicking with imprecations and
commands. To feed grief so
with life and longer grief
is the office of a maniac fortune,
that's generous to a fault.
Out of the dark heart of the earth there bleeds
naptha of honey and hopeless hurt.
Deliver my soul from the sword; my
darling from the power of the dog.
Thou hast given us like sheep
appointed for meat
free among the dead.
Shall thy wonders be known
in the dark?
They came around me daily
like water; they compassed me
about together.
Lover and friend hast thou put
far from me.

Eclogue piece

Cynic

What brings you here
thrice-enamoured man
have I the right to ask?
Here are no efficacious medicines,
strong drink, or trancing weeds,
but the most ordinary of all three,
the fusspots' anodynes.
Grievance or aberration only,
surely, could make you dart
aside here without hope of gain.
I am afraid illusion does not stop
here, at this door. Others may
have gone from here with splints
on phantom limbs, like amputees
one would not let oneself
be disenchanted by;
and some have gone
with some imbalance emphasized
in their conceptions, their conceits;
while the best to come
and the most fortunate if not the best
have rarely left without the exercise
of patience, bounty, firmness
and forbearance. Bitterly I ask
what reason for your call?

Tutor

No trivial inquiry or request
is safe from the vexation it may cause,
but to withhold it sometimes vexes more...
I come to ask you to talk normally.

Nature he loved, and next to Nature, Art

Magic you loved
that magic you shall have
the way I am would last
should this floor turn crag
Beetle browed poet fell on
bed of leaves fell gently poet
the moral heaves freedom freedom
freedom
        that wail must you
create you toffee brain
you rebel-baiter
it's thin toil this season
        and that misapplication of
stress the profane the critic
double lined twister with reason
cur how snarl now freedom
(donated by you Ma'am out of all reason)
with leave to love my bars
snapped cramps with hawk leash
                    deer bray
hound howl and Captains'
tooled brass fanfaroles but
a thin toil this magic and misapplied
    will not be wailed wed walled off or till-rung
                freedom freedom freedom
saith it rained soil
        all schooled tones.

Ripple, bird

Ripple birds it on the shore
peopled by simmering sheep
and the running man skirts
friends come to meet
a fine day ahead of them
Sun lording it over these lives.
Woman crouched in the grass
must have spoken after he passed
to a boat he would have liked it
to have been about mist mornings
the woodpecker and Roman galleys

Gable End

The glitter of a leaf or door, the blackbird's morning raid,
The peaceful life, the leafy lane
The secure roof, the happy times, the perching of a bird
The plates and bowls and frying.

At night the window veiled against the moth
and no-one else
The individual piles of cloth

The sapling towers in the waste
Of railway banks
The butterfly a quiet light
To nod to, thanks

From X

Practically before the sleepy heads rose
to their height on the walls
of many bathrooms, and stores,
there splashed wing streaked
interpreters of the Rose
in cramasy and cobalt
                    /
                on Conway street
Blood had shone
in the mirror of all there
on the Rainbow
on the   sunlit
lizard mourning its tapers.
A blaring laugh
            and some gone
with their   canvas gods
slashed with life-size almond,
                fig-thick
cherry-coated smiles:
god-bellied where sails are
waxing bloom
where a trailing vine
lamplit over and over
        Like apothecaries on stones
        pricking the samphire mud
        apothecaries at the sun-king's levee
        poor sun-king whose soup is always cold
        whose pain is a dry tumult
The small flames tinkle
tumultuous azure laid
            about the bee's track ringing
            round the town in air.

Silver Birch

I also want to tell you about
The tree whose leaves
Always brush my face as I come round
To the back of our house,
And leave a tingling sensation behind
Which goes if there is anyone in
To speak to, for to speak
Is inevitably
To leave a tingling sensation behind
Yet the softness of your voice
From upstairs brushes my eardrums
Like that and is pleasurable
Like that
So that you are the birch tree
And the birch tree is you
In the expenditure of speech then
There is a putting out of leaves
Which like the putting down of roots
Is transitory yet irreversible
Mortal, but spiritual
Just as your hair has gone white -
So - but I go too fast -
I would say the tree, that one
Has known you longer than I have
And you have angled your body in passing
More times than we can count
So, if you did not cut me back,
Would I alter your motions
By growing too close.
Life is a flourish of those branches
They live on light
And the heads that enter their zone
Always different, always debonair.
Live for tomorrow!

Affable

You were a piece of the night, a daytime man
affable, no-one to turn to.
The vinyl turned on the turntable,
the moth displayed in the windowframe.
The day spun by on the analog,
and money changed.

I was a crater of a piece of the night,
askance at the actual tilt of the hill.
The sun failed brilliantly to fill my belly,
And thick smoke filled me with hollowness.
To the day I was an erasion,
and money changed.

I was a night and a day, and a night and a day,
but there is no change of time in a time of terror.
The cloth that covered my creature changed in horror,
The holes in the rags in the mirror dreamt of water.
The day poured into the mirror,
and money changed.

I was a teargas beggar who crept through day,
To a night like yours I could not win or stagger.
The day brought change of place and change of terror,
But no loose change of suffering for better.
Night thoughts of others,
By wars deranged.

The Date

I'm about to embark on a serious relationsh - oops
Spilt orange juice all over my chest,
My narrow chest with stray grey hairs.
Something keeps me excited and happy,
Mainly Shostakovitch tonight,
And the date, October the second,
But really the fair woman telephoned
Who has the face of an elf and the quiet hands
Who speaks to me so that I shall know her
With a sideways look out of hard-won calm,
Who could choose me out of heaven or sheer away,
Calm I said with nothing placid about her,
I will raise a song certainly in her praise
The figure in the tapestry of years.

The Survey

Let there be light: expecting music
He stabbed the radio on, then jabbed it off.
The voice had been bass, transatlantic, brisk
And seemed then to have said quite seriously
"The only map you have is a line of work."
From that you could deduce a scientist,
From that you could begin the work again,
From that you could survey an area
Contouring your own archipelago
Of knowledge and the sunken parts of it.
Taking now as triangulation point
As now no higher ground conceals from you
Your love. Charts, maps, are hand-me-downs,
Inaccuracies featured framed on walls:
One day this present picture will seem naive,
Aesthetic, rough-and-ready, valuable,
Needed as now spread on your lover's floor.

Fairy Liquid

Dreams run down the draining board I sleep
Into the sink of morning. Every hour up
Is a plate heaped with air, I knive and fork
With arms and legs, the daylight seasons
The uneconomical feast of life.
Evenings you draw the cork of work and pour
The old wine of your spirit into my hands.
I baptise the children with a little high indifference,
Let a libation flow to the household gods,
And throw back my head (the wreath falls off).
Garrulous or sunk in meditation
I tell my love in coffee cup words
Darling, sweetheart, I love you,
I cannot find a glass that holds
The sumptuous ocean-varying hues
Of your empowering vintage.
You stack me scoured
In the hot streams of your body
On the gleaming rack of night
Till you rise and the dreams run off.

What was it?

What hit his harried heart amiss
With anguish sharper than the breast?
Emergent from the natal kiss
Desiring only longer rest?

Progenitors of tooth and nail
For all the good they could enjoin
Saw this double helix fail
To grasp the lawful gun and coin,

Flatly despair, and frantically
Issue imperious demands,
Such as "Dismantle family,"
"Take your orders from rock bands."

Later, the doctors asked him in,
Replaced him on the social coil.
He shuffled here and there, to pin
A modest hope in pointless toil.

Health workers without a doubt
With science in their harassed brains
And good volition, had dealt out
sympathy for hidden pains

That music without words would heal
And summers springing with the lark.
Nature and science, both were real
(The nurse of science and nature's clerk,

Now nature's nurse and nature's prison).
Science enhances his unvision
And makes him a more natural person -
At least that is the current version.

Nectar

Now the imperfect silence that follows a backhanded
blasphemy allows dawn as water to flow in the bottleneck
night allowed. Both ways fluid with possibility, and a dry-
mouthed bard poking paper and screen. Possibilities
harden into positions, which raise the leg of necessity
before going out transfixed like the furrows of youth's
flourished browbeating. And quite handsomely dawn falls
on the curtains of the beloved, whose sleep maligns no-
one with these dreams. The interpreters of the sky left last
night seawards, and I looked on and upwards
uncomprehending. Nor has there been a night like this
for lashing at the things that concur in loathing me, in my
home regardless.

Street Corner

The morning lovers on the parapet
besiege with speechless wonders
such as doubt in the time
of ones who pass around
like wind flicks in graveyard grass
parting like curtains on the running boy
parting like scissor blades it seemed
no moment later
on the smoke from Sally's mouth and
leather jacket as she waited for a lift.
What lovers were they, quiet, serious?
What, as he ran, was in the paper bags
he clutched pies maybe, pastries, to eat
after that pear fell by the builders' sand?
The photograph of Sally's grandad's shop
- sweetshop for fags and barber's in the back-
- demolished for the now closed down estate
agents - is no clue to where Sally
went this morning. Only the signature
that's never left by autumn sunlight
the morning lovers and the running boy
gone from our street corner with the wall
left one by one in a sound head
where a door with no-one to close it
hangs open on saplings growing
in the entry to no-one's.

How Pleasant to Meet Mr Trumpet

He always wears a jumper
And never wears a vest
He carries his pyjamas
In case he needs a rest

He smiles at all the passers-by
He never wears a frown
He's such an optimistic guy
He really goes to town

His boots are never polished,
His hat is made of straw,
There is a tomcat visits him
Whose name is Piper Paw

He isn't quite religious
But pagan he is not
His learning's quite prodigious
And his rooms are full of grot

His nose is big, his eyes are moist,
He stoops and he is lean
If he'd only had a daughter
By now she'd be eighteen

If he's walking up the High Street
Dodge him man to man
Or he'll bore you with the stalest news
From Tonga and Japan

And all the while he's talking
He is breathing peppermint
And sticking to his shaving cuts
Are little bits of lint.

Roman

Do I profane these sacred portals with my breath?
Not alone my breath. But my accoutrements
In these rooms are counters of a death
These rooms with no habitués, no clients
No entablature above the porch -
My signs are sword and armour, wine jug, torch.

Here what I did not make I will not mar,
Or strain with analytic meshes -
No gain can make *those* other than they are,
A walking winding sheet and fetishes.

Not while my frenzy freezes to a face,
Can I for long continue in this place
Haunted by spiders and my strange alarms.
I long to take the priestess in my arms.

Watering Duty

While it is true that the arrow-like main street
injecting cars to the admittedly suburban
village, can hide entirely the un-inspected garden

firing valerian, specific for sweats and hysteria,
nursing night-scented stock and near-white irises
and bells, in the borders left by lusty grass

should ivy refuse to clamber the visible gable
end, and the showy clematis be over,
still on the side that does not face the street

A strip of siren summer is in the making.
Such pansies, peonies and pleasant pinks
that hay-fever cannot keep out the tender.

Time of her absence is acceleration
Of what I had thought merely variation

The Smoker Rallies

A practised metronome precludes the hour
from breaking like a wave, inbricks the part
that should be freely weaving like a shuttle
some conscious future. The swathed-in-muscle
heart is cut from query, starts
in a frighted pet. No question does
more than syncopate, reconstitute
the half-dependent breath. No teat
feeds the child forever. This was someone other,
the nectar sickening his throat, the crest
of eyesight on white stubble as he gauged
the scent of glass, and was he worth the bother
to those who sent him loinwards sweet as heather
to punish his own lungs for crying "Mother"?
In texts of pigment and emulsion bound,
in number sets a tethered citizen,
his act is ash always on fire again
and the sky a contusion to fall for tins,
boxes, shrinks, with printed price on skins.
There's not more vision in a central light,
the future has to flicker out of sight.

A Home Opera

The promise is of
Polovtsian dances.

Prince Igor's to the wars.
Prince Galitsky
carouses, forces girls.
The Princess remonstrates, but
bells are heard:
the outskirts of the city are on fire.
The Boyars chorus
"Punishment from God!"

I leave the t.v., go to another room,
large, white, clean, and full
of heritable effects, can hear
the rasp of the producer's voice,
and then, interval over,
a pagan girl is singing to her lover
in the enemy camp.

Let us break out of our captivity!
Let us do something!
But the surge of the music whelms
with the Khan's bass. Is it freedom?
In this house the corridor
reminds me distantly
of a corridor in an asylum
where I could walk free
between the pictures.

As Prince Igor comes home
I have a drawer open in my father's study
and am lifting a box of matches
from under his hunting knife.

It has never laid flesh open
the way it opened a wound in desire
when I took it from its birchwood scabbard
and he gave me sugared rose petals, his boy.

Long live the compassionate Khan! (a killer).
Long live Borodin's broad choruses!
Mother slept through the dances,
and woke up laughing.
The dancers too had subtitles, translating the dance:
the dance we knew of, crazy dance of
happy captives
of the Golden Horde.

The Alliance

The instantaneous logic of the move
made subcutaneous sense, one vomited.
The black queen carrying her war
in close, the count my brother
went looking for a vessel to secure
a leaky and squamous truce.
It is not a bit of use
to sit at anchor biting pipe and nails
and writing to our father bitch in Rome.
But that is what one does, in dull nausea,
on a day of unparalleled splendour,
a hot September day, with the furled sails smelling
of yesterday's rain.
She queered my stomach like a pitchfork,
when I answered her with his absence,
and yet it is not with me she is angry,
but with the gaunt count,
and the fleet he had thought to mount
against our enemies is all around,
rotten and holed and careened for all time.
I have dreamt of her springy breasts
and the black tangled tresses,
but salt is in our wounds,
and they are black too.
As if water could run upwards,
I would have them be friends.

In the Year of the Hurricane

The wind blows in the papery sycamore
Stained leaves that barely meet, they are so few.
The rods branch russet, slant and spindly.
All spring and summer foliage blocked the view
Of ballasted railway tracks in parallel,
Battleship grey gantry holding wires,
Then bank of scrub, pear and magnolia,
The level crossing's white wood kissing gate,
And the new houses. One house built of late
Where there was garden. Monty, old and sly,
Stopped growing spuds when he was widowed,
Let it run wild. One night he did not die
A big wind thrust his wall in on a bed.
"My wife, if she'd been alive," said Monty,
"She'd be dead". Next morning, sunny proof:
The black triangle underneath the roof.
"Monty, the greatest stirrer of them all!"
Is blacked on a wooden spoon at his local.
The bright slight world coherent as a dream
Runs coasting trains across the buried stream
To which the ground slopes, built upon.
Monty, the old reprobate, is gone.

Rumpled

Rescue of an immorality
from virtuous oblivion:
amiably tousle-haired curly haired demon
smiling faintly on the far mist of a miracle
a mirrored time and fast-flowing out.
How this paragon's couple
swivelled her cigaretted head
in a far basin of the bar,
while pugilistic old ladies in the foreground
parcelled out law and caring before midnight.
No saint ever saw such visions of self,
such parodies of an unselved unity,
such splintering placations of longing,
dancing the dark drink down.
The red-haired sunlit loon seen home
and the dog talk-tickled under the jowl
and the cat split-second over the wall of sight
are deprecations of this sliding monologue,
this plucking of hair strings out of the murk
and imageless starings at the hapless vote,
lost without candidate in inebriate glass
and awake to the gloss and the loss of breakfast tv
swayed to from broken bread and bed and bored
with the nightime tune odd lillibulero,
hissle of shortwave tongues riding waves of dialling,
the number my darling of now is now,
the mutiny still talking, still circling stalking
the lifetime of a stopportunity.

Cusp

The sharp cities and the tepid towns
The monkish hoods and academic gowns
Fur hats, thigh boots and daringly bare skin -
I did not think the blanket would be thin.

Jack of All Arts and Waster of None

I paint the vision on the baking tin
A loafer with a canvas belly
Feed me with pastes and bright redcurrant jelly
Hunger the pattern and the origin
Will soon return to cheeses old and smelly.
Provide my need and do not call it greed,
It's gluttony to grind your pepper seed.

Engulfed in Sorrow

The detonations of blisters spill
impotent lymph on scabs of blood.
Good out of evil will not cancel evil.
Shouldering packs of snow civilians arch
February's deceived back into March.
The snow lies desert as Arabian sands,
people are sleeping out like birds and horses
enduring circumstance's enemy forces.
The media fills with war like swollen glands.
Winter jasmine flowers deep in snow.
Before the deaths are set in stone and type
I hope this valentine will help you sniper
To come home soon.

Friend

Slobovitch, my Frankenstein-ish friend
Removes my signature from off the end
Of his petition calling for a war.
He says I don't know what I'm calling for.

I Lay

In the overhanging leaves, sunlight
faded and renewed like humour in things.
Natural lights and cool shade lifted
and swayed on slender rods of understanding.
When a bluebottle buzzes you wait
for it to come back and the waiting,
with a bit of luck, turns to peace.
The glow lights up the leaves
without a sound, as in a sceptical theatre
before the actors filter from the wings
and bubble names and lives and language learned.

Idly wondering

Is it because the day was dark indeed
a man could sit alone and barely read?
The marbled sexton's in the lisping glass
fingering his nose and loosening his collar
and through the hints (the dentist - laughing gas -)
mock the dog-eyes of an intended scholar.

Parable babble

The seed that fell on stony ground was lucky
The leaves were few, the flowers big and pretty.
But what's that smell? The government in waiting
Has laid a light manure about the roots.

Perfect even

The jasmine flowers elfland horns
detach and fall and lightly lie
on leaves of geranium, perfect even
in early dereliction.

Piggy Porker

He gets out through enormous crackinawall,
gains time, recuperates in socks of his own,
then pushes back in, snout and aftershave,
pig naked, curlyhappy, tuskylusty,
and plays piano with tiny trotters.

Emergent Sea

Aroused by ambient salt
the promontory creature nosed for exactness
in the grass
that the dunes produced like fuses of the sand.
The sea lost spray onto it and grew delicate,
grew cold with landlocked tenderness
land laced with droplets of marooned sea,
cast up and claiming the headland dreck
of gravel and bladderwrack and oval stones
of ramwort and stickwit and shellsmell
of barnacleglue and greasefeather and wetflat
of stingwind and dropwet, as witnesses
to the needy seedless propagation motion of water.
But the headland hosed itself down with air
and bucked for nextness to the low down sky
with sea-holly and bulging samphire,
with poppies and bird droppings;
it humped its lowly back and lay there heaving,
lengthening its crusty strand.
Offshore craft
bow away from so much land as that
to the safe sides of their sea
with its slabs of fathom
sea galloping gallons
that salt the point
and leave it streaming.

Song

To free me from a troubling word
That came and meant to stay
She pressed against me in the night
And laughed, and leapt away
I measured with my hand the space
Between us as we lay
I wished our feet always to meet
And drifted through to day.

Spieleology

- not the science of caving
but the study of fast-talking
delivery immured in the cave of echoes
has made me more convinced than - was I ever? -
that being lost for words is a still more telling
condition of the heart. Some phenomena
simply cannot grow in a culture of verbiage,
which are beautiful in a new-minted silence.
When there is no communication for days
the subtlest attention is possible.
The flow of love is resumed, purified,
in the moments before the return of chatter.
Picking a horny callous off my foot
this bit of me is dead, detached. It's thought
the self's a husk, discarded soon as spoken.
What rubble, when the egg of self is broken.

John the Adaptist

The charm school was finished with him
ignorantly wise

about how to please
with the least surprise

and a crowd came down to the water
to see him baptise

but they only stood about foolishly
while he sprinkled a few drops on a dog and shouted

I can see it in your eyes!

Get the hem of your garments wet, my dear crowd
in a moment the dredger is passing by in buckets
and a scum of strawberries bobs upon the foam.

Your old god won't do, the young sun god,
or the god before last either who was obligatory,
neither plain nor adorned wisdom you have heard
nor sensitive common sense from within, no,
you want me to sprinkle you
like one of your own lawns
till your hairs sprout green with seedling happiness
and your brain drips with copious freedom
and your tongue runs with truthful words again.

Sorry, nothing doing.
Will the civilized lascivious censor
who is knowing and wise with the lash and the curb
kindly supervise the dispersal,
after we've had
our swim?

Little Johnny's Concession

The collector of impossible love-lyrics
goes on the road? By road? Well, on a by-road
and finds a Fordson tractor trying
to monkey about with a strapless Massey- Ferguson,
says one, it is not impossiblefor a man to love a tractor:
only
for the tractor to which he was attracted to return
that love which furrows his brow and is fatal to metal
it would have to turn its man to metal
and make him more mobile, more malleable.
No tractor I know has the heart for that.
And so, sick for the field-workers' metamorphosis,
we vainly try in all gears to trespass our trade-marks,
negate our name-plates,
forget the factories that made us
 - they do not own us now - and left to rust
by disappointing late-enlightened swains,
we leave the furrows to the hare and cock-pheasant
and mingle our parts till our motors pink.
The skies, rust-colour, turn to indigo
the moon rises empty, like our tanks,
and then wispy traces of Zodiac
like scattered sparking plugs.

Myth

The youth throwing stones all afternoon
chucking stones
chukkies
chipping away at the peace
peace fretted with whirlwinds of chatter
frittering chatter.
Wind in the corn making the dry stalks rustle.
How many bold footprints can the dust hold?
The cattle were sunk on folded knees,
on grounded haunches, every cow
too apathetic to stir.
The boy pushing along the path
butting on against all others
heeding the maternal a little.
A little stay in the woods,
the boy jumping the stream
brandishing tree trunks
raising and dashing
jumping the dead clear stream.

Briefly on the same ground
the same mystic stance
the maiden waving arms
in a slight dance
to music of her own mouth.

The women of my age converse
at ease in the place's peace.
My head aches and I want to crush them all
I need to go and take a paracetamol
at home and quietly recall
the hellish bluebell dell.

Getting Away

Is it so strange that I should walk at night
the shining river bank, up Cut-Throat Lane,
along the roadside back across Bowes' fields?
Perhaps surprising that I did go back,
being so angry, to the waiting ones.
That was it: waiting. I inscribed a curse
inwardly, in case of need of it,
and it invoked the anger without cause
which made me rise and say "I'm going out!"
as if not needed, as the curse was not.
And yet, to formulate it, like a wish -
a mousetrap in the hold-all for a thief,
a piled-up cloud upon a sunny plain,
alarm-clock set for the wrong time of night -
I did not know how to de-activate,
dissolve the curse within the cottage walls,
so had to get away. The snapping rod,
the thunderstorm, the dream-impacting bell
all eased to the rest state with observant pacing,
abstinence, industry and continence.
But why the wish, the playful condemnation?
"If you won't eat the food I give you, starve!"
It bears an atavistic connotation.
Playful? It reeks of wrangles in the cave!
Who with the power to give and to withhold
but fears indifference like the loss of gold?

From Alresford Creek

Where a boat goes round on a rope
the bright and dark sides alternate, combine
like floating phases of distorted moon
and you could be modelling the figures
of ellipses wagging, tugging on the buoy
but sit rapt and alert before the shell...
A scene from Ithaca, Telemachus watching,
and for the weaving loom and suitors din
a workday grinding and a clank inland
and independent sopranino twitters.
A kite in the sky is
drawn down on a line to the sunlit prey.
As a runner takes the winding lane of may
the sheep in heaven are bleating for their feed
but he is turning from the sea to the bluebells
cruel, crockery blue
from bluebells to the brimful estuary
where small oak leaves tuft twigs the brightest green
and gorse is golden on the warmest side.
Erosion has made unrecognisable inroads
a hollow treetrunk has been swallowed whole
but still eyebrow branches of tamarisks
stoop looking leafless to the tide that is come,
water without the river's brown suspension
from depths of ocean tiptoed in
to lap that dryhard bank below the path.
And here the fluid footsteps beach on gravel
an aggravating sound, and far behind,
as the hawk eats entrails,

- the boat fetches round.

Triptych 1

Was he ever any
thing, the sour-skinned dosser
swigging bravado
on a town-centre wall?
He has company, no cleaner
but less drunk, he has what looks like
leisure to discuss and gossip:
so far, like others -
though some are lonelier
in towers of sufficiency.
Was he ever known to us
by name, and avoided
for the flint in his eye
and the nettling speech,
who now mocks us
in our anonymity
from his ragged citadel
of public space?

In a quiet moment I seem to see
his satellites depart,
taking his bravado with them.
Yellow-eyed and slack-toothed
he gets moody, argumentative, yelling.
Violently, with bile in his mouth,
he is kicked to death by agents
of the no-smoking-in-public state,
and charges are dropped,
or never brought
against his assailants.
But no not that.
He's thinly propped
in the little garden like space
meant for civility

not bold distress.

Passing by with lives
he wouldn't want
we're all moving morons
to his paralytic highness.
Don't let's be one big objection:
he is the surface of an iceberg
idly summoning up courage
to walk, and stop the Titanic traffic.

Walton to Frinton

Walking the beach companionably fast
in warm and hazy sunlight keeping pace
on sandy ribs and multi-coloured stones.
till looking down, the sharp cut edge of sand.
Water that coiled and bucked and shone
in a run made straight by a buried groyne.
It seemed to say we had come far enough.
Turning we saw the afternoon lagoon,
its surface plucked with flutters, flat with the wind's

                                           power.
We had come round from one town to the next
a neat distinction ignored by the sea,
as if, having locked a hut, we needed boatfuls of air.
Our words flowed with us, wisely tolerant,
as if some meaning kept back from before
like that pool's waters farther up the beach
had reached the present with surprising force.

Conversation

Now the trilling has stopped in the tree,
raising the eyes to note the place,
it's there I see
the sparrow and that other
life-sized bird of glass
that sits at the crossing
of the window-frame and boughs.
The live one seems to talk
and talk is cheap
the glass one listens and glistens
surely it's not paranoid?
By the tilting of the head
ye shall know the living
outlasting the image as a species does – and still
the heavy, rounded blob of silica
transparently says
bird, I symbolize
& though I cannot fly at will,
I sit and sing of taking wing.

The End of the World

An ivy and a spiderplant descend
 From off the mantelpiece at either end.
The fireplace holds some withered purple blooms,
There's no-one home in any other rooms.
Vivid pansies in the window box
Bob in the sun well past the equinox.
Sun patches paint a lampshade, a hi-fi,
A book or two, a sewing tin. The spy
Sees how all pass the council notice board
Not stopping still to read. Uphill, the Lord
has churches' posters that don't say
Ussher predicted this as the last day.
Then some do stop to look at public bills
and find them lacking Armageddon's thrills
and for a while
one notices their gender or hair-style.
These figures from transitional cyber-games
switch to walk-past-it mode and stream downhill
(one reaches absent-minded for a pill)
but they retain in private certain names
between themselves and God - Whose history
cautions with Bishop Ussher's prophecy

Looking

As I get older I don't know
what it's for, the city-building
the road-running the treaty-making
hostages voyages intaglio light relief
a quiet bedroom autumn sunlight
penetrating entanglement of
branches, clematis twists
and curtain lace it may be
that if I slept out I would know
more deeply or differently
the bale, the bias of the world
I submit with a dark
countenance looking to the trials of time
for some enduring romance. Alabaster
and carnations! The irony is
time is spacious and holds us briefly
within its radiant iris with all else
and even before we are dust -

Strolling

- blinking, down the avenues of illusion
groups of cramps and congeries of grimaces
acknowledge the onset of evening with hard smiles,
shuffles, and outstretched arms: the Dordogne,
the Grand Canyon, Novaya Zemblaya,
wherever you thought you would go it is here now
in the lamp-lit crevices of the communal blancmange
that Mr Oatmeal pulls a long face and Mrs Wit bares
                                                    teeth,
here more beards wag together on a claim of right
than birds sing under the gutter in a curry-house's eaves,
and one fine fisherman jammed in the window seat
holds conference with a kind of man three sheets to the
                                                    wind
before the last train bears away on its syncopated bogies
a scattering of weary human cargo
casting a gleam on the mysterious country dark
of sheep and barley, poppies and chamomile
after mile after mile after mile and all
the dreams trail like odoriferous scarves
unwinding from the scabby scalp of daytime
unable to alight and hold a pint here
as the evening unevenly eventuates
in the streets of another town.

Emergencies

She's in one already, looking round for help
or for antagonists who leap and learn.
She's crossing the road, looking around,
as you do, at junctions, even you
if you remember, Mr Sombrero.
Insurgencies in the family
she emerges from wholly transformed,
unhappily transfixed by the performance,
feeling what her hair and teeth tell her:
older is a state of affairs, not mind.
What can we do, dear woman, slipping past
on urgencies not so bereft as yours
but ask if healing's in the gift of time
although you say our lives are on the line.

Ulysses

Listening here: voices of exposition, urgent news,
banter of entertainment, intonations,
expressive comment, discussion of the young,
songs sung in the shower and on the stairs.
I want to talk about the salt sea-spray
cast on a windscreen like a heavy net,
cast on, rubbed off and wrapped again,
while an engine drones on somnolently.
No-one speaks and night is coming on.
Where is the gangway you anticipate,
the slap under a keel, bow bobbing, groans,
the cable with its loop a booted man
slips from the capstan and hoys off-land;
hoots, and a churning screw, the radar sweep
whose traces glow and fade, repeatedly?
There's no course onward over reef and wreck.
So make no more of capes and beacons, make
a paper hat and sail it in the bath,
wonder who made one for you once,
what have the years been caterpillars for,
that were set afloat upon nasturtium leaves
(or now you imagine)
in young days long ago.

The Tendency to Exaggeration

Fifteen, and he has fished that pond for years
on moonlit nights, on any night, whenever:
he would just go and stay there days
on the long wooded path that links the pegs
where there's another boy's memorial bench
facing the cliff that darkens first at eve,
that boy who fished and mapped the lake, its depths
and features, fringed with youngish oaks, who died.
The island by which grebes train up their young
is where a heron sometimes can be seen.
Our lad with "fish-in-arms" is happiest,
putting them back alive though torn at lip.
The gravel pit was his enchanted scene.
He never called it beauty. Loved it there.
And now, nearby, he thinks, they've dug another, hit
the water table, caused much of the lake
to drain away. Today he and the club
are rescuing the fish - carp, tench and bream
and maybe perch and roach though not the pike
to move them to a raw and ugly water hole
not big enough to hold them. End
of a boy's idyll. Greed of men
destroys a world of beauty. So next year
he thinks he'll fish off the M25.

Beetle Rampant

Better than war
this world's natural industry, its work
pouring forth butterflies galore
putting horns on cows, leaving many a mark.
So many

Made gates close against tides but take
the stag beetle hovering heraldically
heart-high in a path that footsteps make
between the feverfew and spires of nettle.
It inspires.

Heavy rains made a mess of the barley
but in a thicket of oak and holly, birch and chestnut
there is a pond supporting ducks that rarely
panic at a man's foot on the moss
or brute.

Mowing

I went mowing but the blade caught fire
Poured away the fire water but it caught
In my throat. I am only doing what I ought.
But I must put me up for hire
Deferring my entire desire
In a continuum of showing
Fight in the interests of a thought

At last I swallow my indignity

The blunder boy and renegade
        I wake up by the tumble dryer.

Away with Touch, the subtle liar,
And Sight, the biggest egotist,
Every active sense exists
Linked to reaction that persists
In wreaking havoc.

Peace shall be
     Calm and quiet thought
Then to meditation brought.
Ardent
As poetry my head was clear -
Head-first I fell into my beer!
Tobacco, too, is on the list:
I am another, who resists
The vices on which I insist.

The Image of Herself

Radiantly lovely, she dressed herself
facing the mirror, for a day at work.
Her wet hair, tangled in a clinging weave,
hung heavy round her neck so fine.
Then in the bathroom, when I stood behind her,
and held her waist, she dodged from side to side,
asking, did I want her, or the mirror?
Her hair was dry by then, and like a poem,
except the lines went down and not across.
The mirrors glisten all day facing loss,
and they upbraid me with not keeping her.

Utopia for Two

The courts decide which children may get married,
The holy man dispenses quick divorces,
Mothers by their babies shall be carried,
And Love the author be of all discourses.

This shall be when no dispute arises
About inheritance or custody
Happiness shall be quick with our surprises
And music have no need of melody

Soft Soap - a Light Comedy

Thorny winds and lashing rain
Part my dry and damaged hair
Products of Nature's cold and wild campaign
For which a good coat is the best conditioner

In the street outside your house I had this shower
To which your cutting words consigned my head
And shoulders. But it's in your power
To loosen locks which hang on me like dread.

But should your wintry discontent continue
And you still toss your head at your true friend
I'll join another beauty's ardent retinue
and hang upon another girl's split ends

I hope it doesn't come to that infringement dear
I've shoulder-length fidelity to you
Your soft and silky looks will always win me dear
And curly laughter all the Springtime through.

Her Reply

Threats and inducements do not win me over
You dandruff-stricken individual!
And what inducements? I have blown your cover
It's you who paint me to the world as cruel.

Slosh on the two-in-one stuff all you want to
And here is an elastic band or two
I'm really sorry I don't mean to taunt you
But I can't fall in love with a shampoo.

Winter

The trains pass by in waterfalls of sound
Distant gunshots puff against the ear
Every feeling person has gone to ground
And drawn the duvet over the calendar

The Year is throwing at us wheeling starlings
Snowberries dangle by the bridge and brook
Eyes looking into mine are not my darling's
And instead of real work I cook

Debris lies about the door. That roses
Bloom in December occasions some surprise.
Sores are healed with timed and stated doses
Of wisdom manufactured under early skies.

A passing train of thought is soon distracted
A gunshot wound is foully to be borne
Life is a river, wrong thoughts too soon acted,
Change is in all: so darling, change your scorn

Oh, I Believed

Sling the tedium and crap and let sun shine
in offices and classrooms where rules cramp
spontaneous affinity and children whine
the summer grass is cut the ground is damp

where they sat in circles playing cards
and swearing gruffly never to grow old
or too old to be seen in leotards
repeating the illusions they were sold

too old, too young to wake at six o'clock
baking with pleasure in the double bed
aching with dread of working hours that lock
the spirit in a straightjacket of lead

Oh, to grow wise with joy and cleverness
and free the body in a flood of calm!
Oh I believe that all is lost unless
I praise the symbol hidden in your palm!

The Scorner at Heartache

You sat astride the carriage like a hayseed gone to pot,
And stuck a leg in denim out to brake hard with your
                                                boot.
It was a lovely train of thought that had nowhere to stop
Like the man's who saw the seagull fly and let his body
                                                drop.
My throat got dry with thinking first of Rimbaud then of
                                                vin,
Of how d sounds in silence and I almost rhymed with am.
Oh the ambushes of amity – there never was another
In the complicity of hate who wrote like little Arthur.
And now you think that John will leave the sea and go to
                                                Jesus,
A dream that reads, an ear that speaks, a willing heart
                                        that frees us.

Elegy for W.B.

Dear father, if you are not gone
Into the fields of asphodel
Leaving your tenement of bone
As clappers of an ashen bell

Are you not gone to Tir nan Og,
The islands of eternal youth
To feel no cares and keep no log
Of deviations from the truth,

Are you not jesting with the saints
Who share the keys of heaven's skies,
Knowing joy without constraints,
Facing God with glad surprise?

The gardens of Persephone
Are all around us. Mourning you
We, your surviving colony
Remember twinkling eyes of blue

And how you had sagacity,
Humour, warmth and intellect.
Profound was your capacity
To render and to win respect.

"No more!" the organ shall pibroch.
No more your mouth will firmly tell
The names of moor and ben and loch!
Nevermore dear William Bell!

Elegy for Douglas Leslie

Open-minded, principled, compassionate,
In a high-minded Scottish kind of way
Unfooled; benevolent and humorous
How Dickens would have loved you!
How the airs of frequent walks would often
Lift your mood and tangle your fine hair.
You kept your figure but in your affections
Were never lean or mean. A man of parts
With friends in every *airt*, and friend to nature,
At home with Muslim, Christian, Hindu, Jew.
There was a gentle wonder in your speech,
Thinking yourself so fortunate and yet
Deafness was *wersh*, and overcoming that
Was hard – yet you were eminent.
Your good luck was in fact to be
Yourself and to be loved. Douglas the brave,
Your merits live forever. The effects
Of goodness go on acting in the world
Even when all who knew the man are dead.
So while we live and breathe, be cheered by this,
And by the thought of Douglas in his trews.

Armchair Critic

The speech the wind makes in the trees
Is many mock soliloquies:
A hundred actors playing Lear
To one spectator shut in here
On a sofa's cushioned stuff
While the green room has it rough.
The one is many, in a storm
With scarce a limit, scarcely form,
But all is one, the one alone
Inside a hollow megaphone.
The tossing mane of foliage
Is stricken nature on the stage,
His upright trunk resists the gale
Nor suffers yet the saw and nail:
Concentric rings this actor's lines
Uncut until the tree reclines.
Shaking his noble head the mast
Shall bring the storm to peace at last,
And all his peers at the same time
Shall bring the curtain down in rhyme
Of raindrops slipping through their leaves,
Which no-one now but me conceives.
The silent dripping actors stand
In a housed and sheltered land
But the homeless peeping out
From blankets put the end in doubt,
The speech the wind makes in the trees
Brings power lines to pylons' knees
And in the theatre of fate
Nature weeps a wilder state.

The Stage

How we admire the passion and the anger
That make the drama's tragic sweep unfold
And let the audience, that motley ogre,
Hide in the very horrors they behold:
Hysteria, discord, hope and disillusion,
Slapstick, and a makeshift sympathy
United us in search of a solution
To lack of recognition, apathy,
The isolation shared we all endure.
It made you smile, for all of us were poor.
The ghost of Hamlet's father on the turrets
No longer sends a shiver down our spines,
We judge the old pretender on his merits.
The players have learnt other, softer lines,
The ladies look at us through fingers sly;
"There's just the one rehearsal, and we die".

Absence, Presence

Absence and presence, resin on the strings,
Wind in the reed and spout, you drum my heart,
Wanting to see the morning light that brings
Nature to life, and splits the dark apart.
Parted clouds that shine above the rout.
Doubt is uncertain too, faith in a root,
In birdsong, in the tree, in falling fruit.

Also in the halting song is a harsh mixture
Of toppled architecture, broken fixture
Appalled appraisal and stark apprehension.
Evening sighs with daylong trawl of tension.
Let go into a night of silent dream
Waking in sleep a native-alien theme

Flight is unthinkable: but let us fly
Stop the flute, quick fingers, let us try
To raise a melody and hear it die
Before us. Life is fluid, books are dry.
The flock will wheel together in the light
Birds perch and sing and swoop, alight and bite.

Flowers do sense our presence; trees grow tall
To teach humility; the rains that fall
May fall too heavily, or not at all

Epithalamium

There is a planet Earth not Googled and gazetted
Not parcelled into plots and policed, not
Fenced off for the famous
An earth that is green beyond measure,
The earth we love to stand on,
Where the May Queen and her maidens hold sway,
And a king of men in his way, if he is handsome,
courageous and strong,
Light-hearted and true, reigns equally, rewarded with joys
Which last past summer, with love and a quiet heart
That stays and plays through winter days,
Love quickening the heart and soul of life
For these two persons beyond comparisons,
Gus and Miranda,
Each answering the other's fire and spark,
Each is the other's sanctuary and ark,
These two rare beauties, whose hearts tally
In the loving struggle, the meeting, the fusing of passions
to hard ruby rocks of fidelity.
These whom we love are joined now in promise and
pledge
And we are here to witness and willingly rejoice in your
wild and wonderful wedding.

The Reason There Is Everywhere

Feather fixed in air.
Barely visible, the catenary curve
Of a fine thread flung
From stem to stem by a hungry spider.
The feather rested there
From its brief ecstasy of detachment.

Elegy for Joan Nevard

How I shrink from the task, my muse, o you must
                                                  help
Me say what only can be said in sad lament
With zealous faith, which bitterness forbids,
Unworthy I begin, whom you inspire,
With loyal love to help my faltering flight,
To hymn the memory of this lady dear,
And sweep solemnity from its dread throne
As she did often, smiling ear to ear.
As she advised, pomposity would flee
And common sense, oft hand in hand with glee,
Would sit with kindness and shrewd sympathy.
What helped a child was what she championed,
What remedy was best she'd advocate,
Or to conceive be first. Beauty she loved,
In children, birds and flowers, she was the most
Delighted witness of their innocence,
Defender of their faith, and mother love
Love and instruction, were her attributes.
Such pretty ways herself, she had, to find
Joy like a girl in taking cake and tea
With those she loved, rising above the cares
Sown deep by tragedies in early years.
From child to working girl in wartime Leeds
A concert-going, witty, worthy lass
Without a father's love, brave as a man,
To southern marriage, children by the sea,
And forging lasting friendships. Active years
Of nurturing and learning, generously
Extending friendly hands to Germany,
Summers of travel and discovery.
Happy with books and songs and grandchildren,
She gave love outward, mingled in the mass

And took a human interest in all. At last,
Her memories focused further in the past,
She firmly held her ground and loved the more
Her own sweet children. How can she be gone?
How calm she is, who lived so nervously.
At peace is Joan, who sturdily contended.
Though she be sleeping still when dawn arrives,
Long shall she live in stories and in lives.
What can she see beyond the chestnut trees?
No more sorrow, suffering or disease.
Let tears be shed, but wipe away their flood,
Her spirit's with you each time you do good,
Her humour will be with you when you laugh,
Her brightness shine within you when you help
Anyone weaker, anyone in pain,
This brave and kindly woman is in heaven,
Teaching the little angels seven times seven
And writing letters to the Paradise Council.

Daybreak midnight

Darkness fell on the road home
and everything seemed a bit clearer
for the rumble underneath and the driving
            rain not falling today
                        in the sun
he and I through trees and past
A towering single pylon
the path led into woods and out, a gate then
spongy 'ground' and the triangular sprung
see-saw that needs no other. He
rocked, swung, slid & spun.
Teazles by the sub-station fence
luckily no dogs anywhere
later that rangy Dalmatian
distracted from photos of underground stations
"Details being all you can picture
without the stuff in front - cars mostly -"
On the road home, I learnt, a nasty accident
though all I'd heard was the flashing
blue lights and yellow stripes
I started the day "incredibly sympathetic"
So cold that night so quiet

www.ingramcontent.com/pod-product-compliance
Lightning Source LLC
Chambersburg PA
CBHW051005050726
47592CB00007B/2720